HOW TO DRAW DINOSAURS

Illustrated by
Georgene Hartophilis

MALLARD PRESS

An Imprint of BDD Promotional Book Company, Inc.
666 Fifth Avenue
New York, N.Y. 10103

Mallard Press and its accompanying design and logo
are trademarks of BDD Promotional Book Company, Inc.

First published in the United States of America
in 1991 by The Mallard Press

ISBN 0-7924-5568-1

Introduction

This book will show you some easy ways to draw lots of different dinosaurs. Some may be more difficult than others, but if you follow along, step-by-step, you'll soon be able to draw any dinosaur you wish.

Using the basic shapes illustrated below will help you get your drawing started. Remember that these shapes, in different sizes and combinations, will change from dinosaur to dinosaur. Variations of these shapes will also be used.

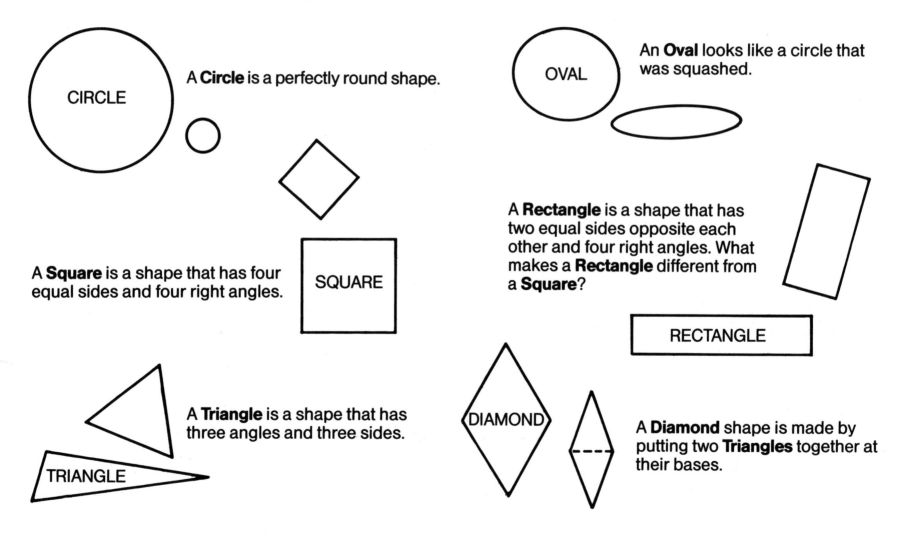

A **Circle** is a perfectly round shape.

An **Oval** looks like a circle that was squashed.

A **Square** is a shape that has four equal sides and four right angles.

A **Rectangle** is a shape that has two equal sides opposite each other and four right angles. What makes a **Rectangle** different from a **Square**?

A **Triangle** is a shape that has three angles and three sides.

A **Diamond** shape is made by putting two **Triangles** together at their bases.

Supplies

NUMBER 2 PENCILS
SOFT ERASER
DRAWING PAD
FELT-TIP PEN
COLORED PENCILS, MARKERS,
   OR CRAYONS

Helpful Hints:

Before starting your first drawing, you may want to practice tracing the different steps. Start your drawing by lightly sketching out the first step. The first step is very important and should be done carefully. The second step will be sketched over the first one. Next, refine and blend the shapes together, erasing any guidelines you no longer need. Add final details and when your drawing is complete, go over your pencil lines with a felt-tip pen. If you wish, you may color your drawing with markers, pencils, or crayons.

Each dinosaur has special characteristics that make it easier or, in some cases, more difficult to draw. However, it's easy to draw anything when you break it down into simple shapes! Remember, practice makes perfect, so keep drawing until you've mastered each dinosaur. Use your imagination. Experiment with color; create different dinosaur scenes; and most of all, HAVE FUN!

Apatosaurus

(a-PAT-oh-SAWR-us)

Means "Deceptive Lizard." It is also known as Brontosaurus.

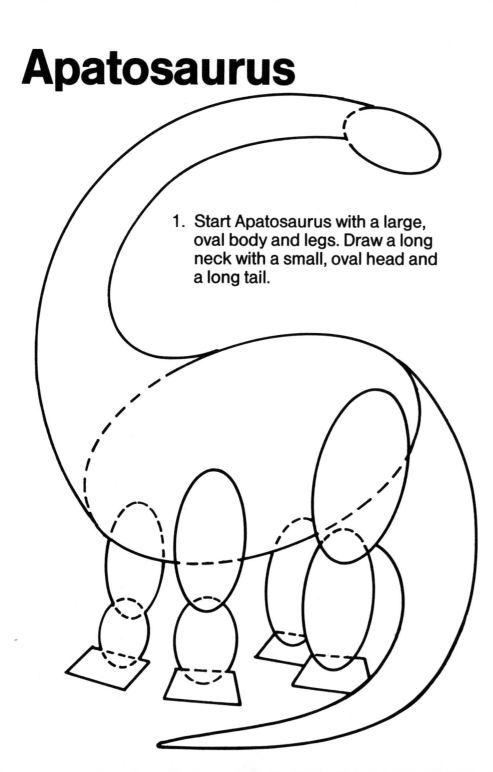

1. Start Apatosaurus with a large, oval body and legs. Draw a long neck with a small, oval head and a long tail.

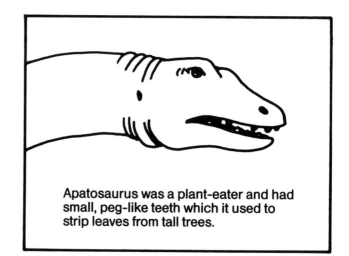

Apatosaurus was a plant-eater and had small, peg-like teeth which it used to strip leaves from tall trees.

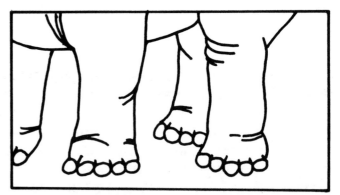

Apatosaurus had thick feet and legs. Its footprints measured nearly 36 inches long and 26 inches wide!

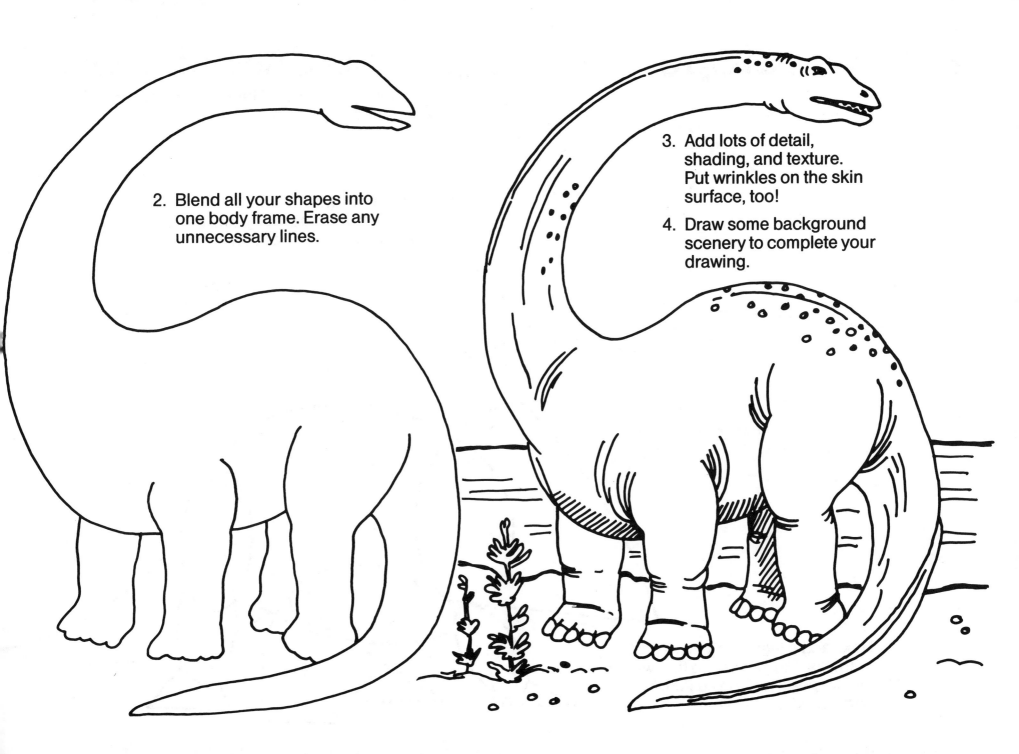

2. Blend all your shapes into one body frame. Erase any unnecessary lines.

3. Add lots of detail, shading, and texture. Put wrinkles on the skin surface, too!

4. Draw some background scenery to complete your drawing.

Protoceratops

(pro-toe-SAIR-uh-tops)

Means "First Horned Face" because this was one of the first horned dinosaurs.

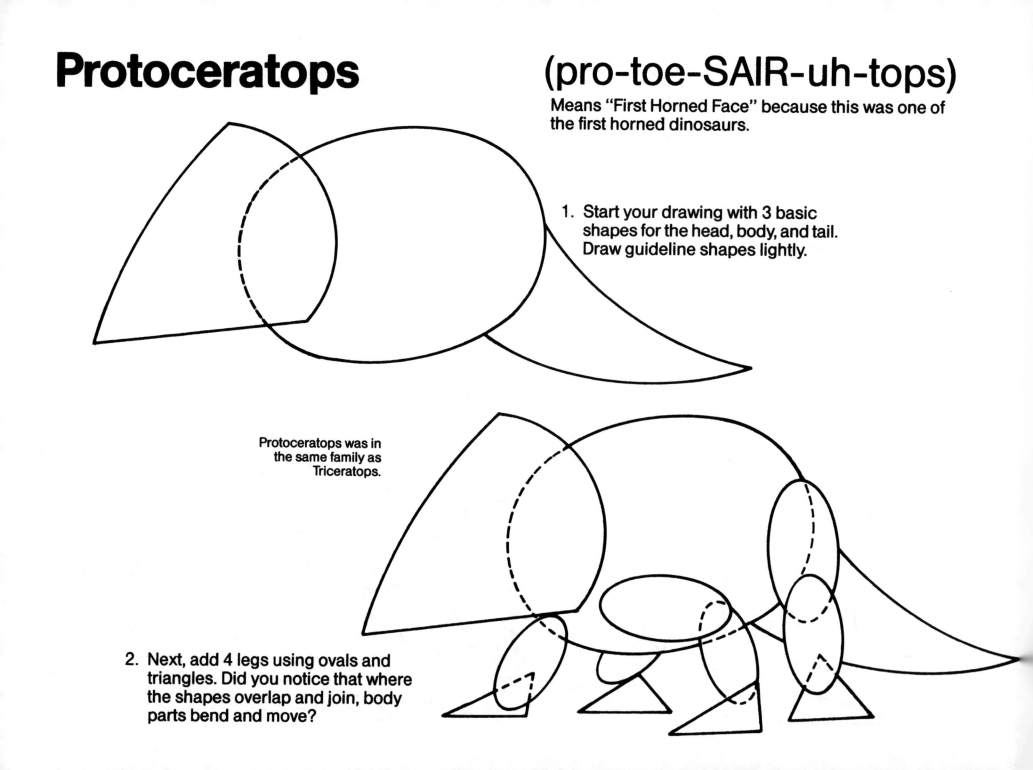

1. Start your drawing with 3 basic shapes for the head, body, and tail. Draw guideline shapes lightly.

Protoceratops was in the same family as Triceratops.

2. Next, add 4 legs using ovals and triangles. Did you notice that where the shapes overlap and join, body parts bend and move?

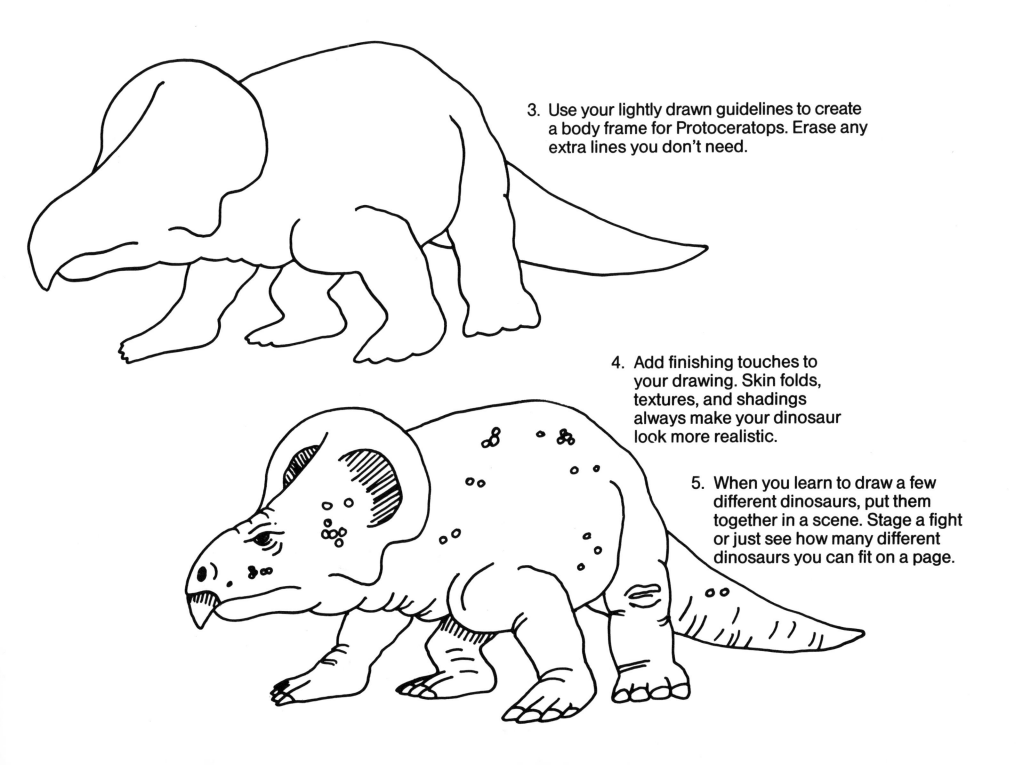

3. Use your lightly drawn guidelines to create a body frame for Protoceratops. Erase any extra lines you don't need.

4. Add finishing touches to your drawing. Skin folds, textures, and shadings always make your dinosaur look more realistic.

5. When you learn to draw a few different dinosaurs, put them together in a scene. Stage a fight or just see how many different dinosaurs you can fit on a page.

Maiasaura

(mah-ee-ah-SAWR-ah)

Means "Good Mother Lizard" because most scientists believe this dinosaur stayed with and cared for her offspring.

1. Lightly draw a large oval body, long neck, and a small oval head.

2. Next, add a tail and four legs. Three legs are fully drawn, but the fourth leg is partially hidden behind another.

3. Blend your guidelines and shapes into a body frame. Erase any lines you don't need.

4. Add lots of details. Draw an eye, claws, nostril, skin folds, textures, and shadings.

5. Draw Maiasaura in a scene standing guard over her nest of eggs.

Corythosaurus

(KO-RITH-uh-sawr-us)

Means "Helmet Lizard" and refers to the shape of the bony crest on its head.

1. Start your dinosaur drawing with basic shapes (ovals and circles) for the head, neck, and body. These are only guidelines, so draw them in lightly.

2. Next, add guidelines for the tail, legs, arms, and mouth. The Corythosaurus had a mouth that looked like a duck's and large, powerful legs to support its body.

   Hint: dotted guidelines will be erased, so draw them lightly.

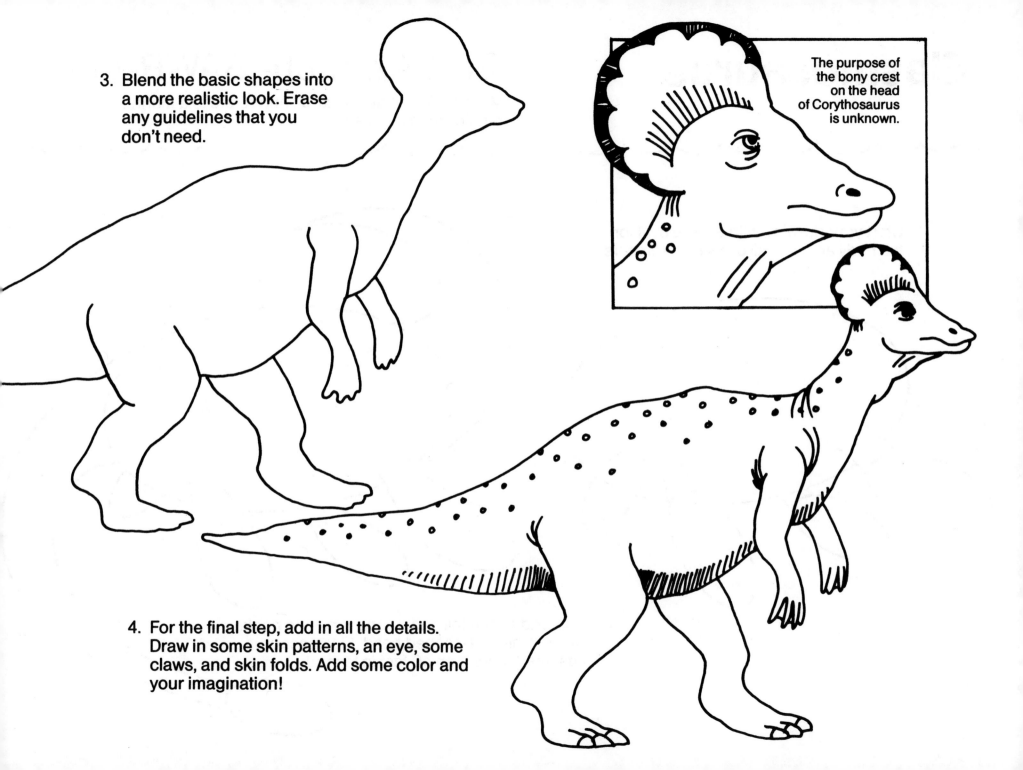

3. Blend the basic shapes into a more realistic look. Erase any guidelines that you don't need.

The purpose of the bony crest on the head of Corythosaurus is unknown.

4. For the final step, add in all the details. Draw in some skin patterns, an eye, some claws, and skin folds. Add some color and your imagination!

Elasmosaurus

(ee-LAZ-muh-SAWR-us)

Means "Thin-plated Lizard" and refers to a marine
reptile, not a dinosaur.

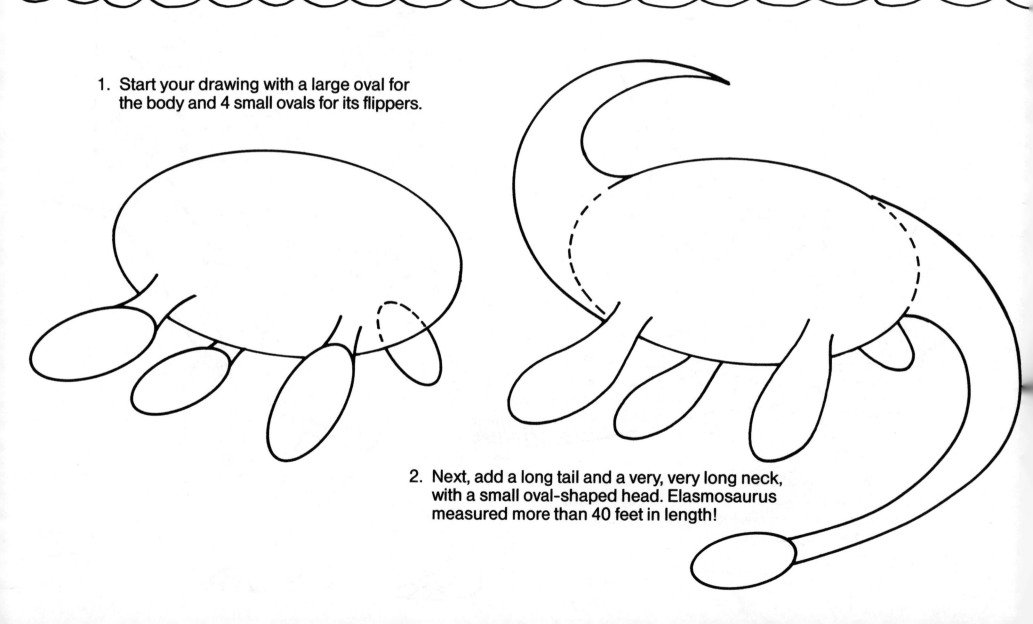

1. Start your drawing with a large oval for
   the body and 4 small ovals for its flippers.

2. Next, add a long tail and a very, very long neck,
   with a small oval-shaped head. Elasmosaurus
   measured more than 40 feet in length!

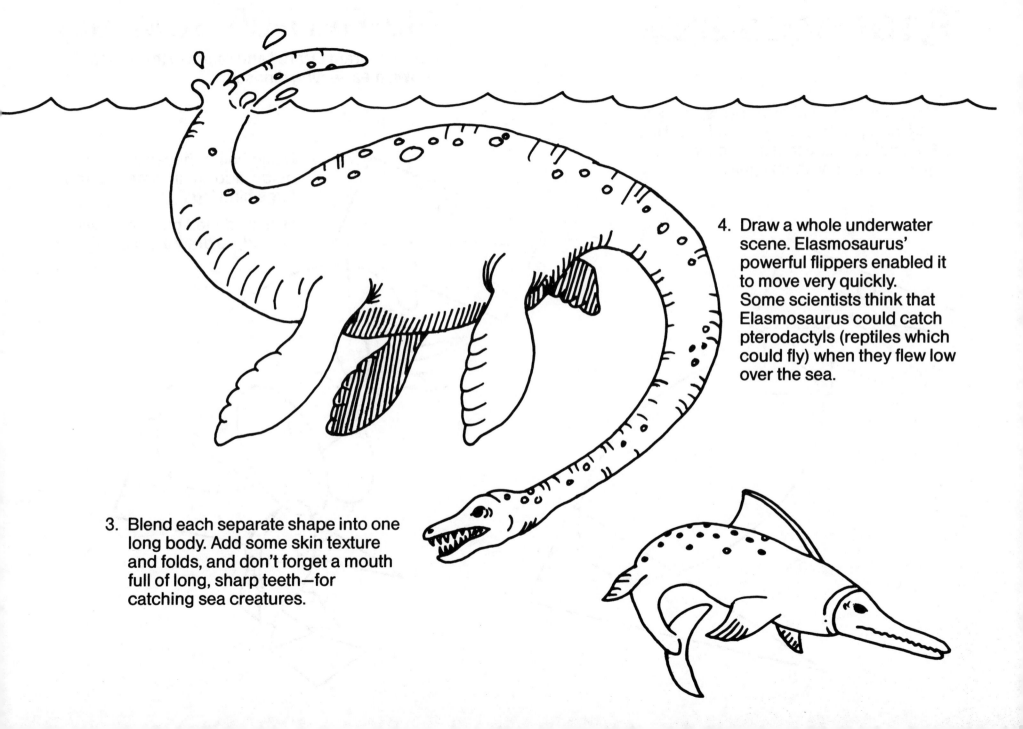

4. Draw a whole underwater scene. Elasmosaurus' powerful flippers enabled it to move very quickly. Some scientists think that Elasmosaurus could catch pterodactyls (reptiles which could fly) when they flew low over the sea.

3. Blend each separate shape into one long body. Add some skin texture and folds, and don't forget a mouth full of long, sharp teeth—for catching sea creatures.

Tyrannosaurus

(tie-RAN-uh-sawr-us)

Means "Tyrant Lizard" and refers to the largest known meat-eating dinosaur.

1. Use rectangles, squares, ovals, circles, and triangles for the head, body, and tail. Remember, since these are only guidelines, draw them lightly.

2. Using basic shapes as your guide, add small forearms and large hind legs.

   Hint: all dotted guidelines will be erased, so draw them extra lightly.

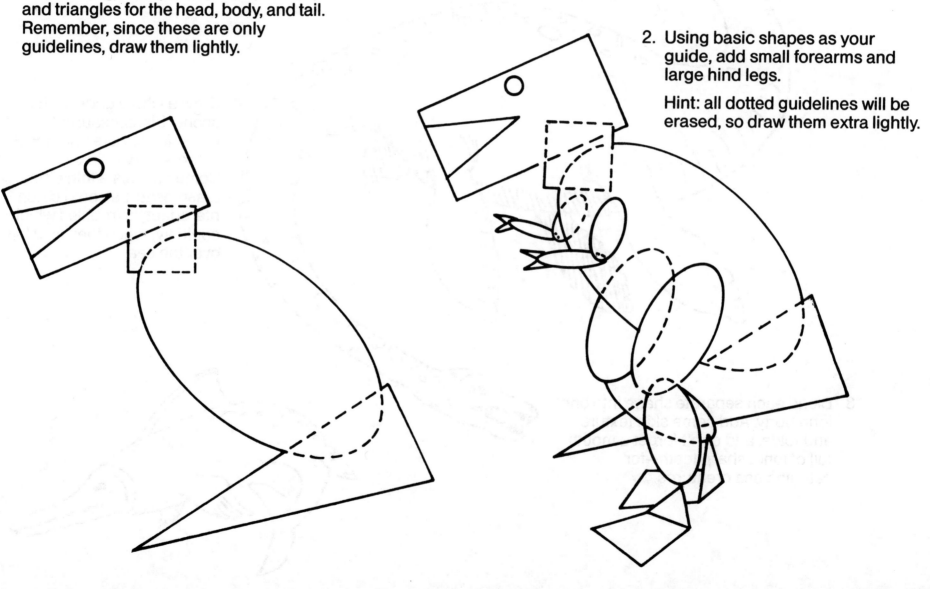

3. Use your guidelines to draw the basic body shape. Don't forget to erase any lines you don't need.

4. Put all the finishing touches on your drawing. Give Tyrannosaurus a more ferocious look, big teeth, a mean look in its eye, and lots of skin effects. What color do you think Tyrannosaurus was? No one really knows, so let your imagination run wild!

Hint: once you learn to draw different dinosaurs, make a whole dinosaur scene!

Ankylosaurus

(an-kee-luh-SAWR-us)

Means "Stiffened Lizard" and refers to its hard armor-plated body surface.

1. Start your Ankylosaurus with a large oval body. Use ovals as guidelines for its four legs. Use triangles for its feet.

2. Next, add a long triangle for its tail with an oval on the end. Don't forget to add some triangle shapes for "spikes" all over its back.

3. Erase any guidelines you don't need. Add more bumps to its armor-plated back.

4. Now finish your drawing by adding claws to the feet, an eye, bumpy skin, and more!

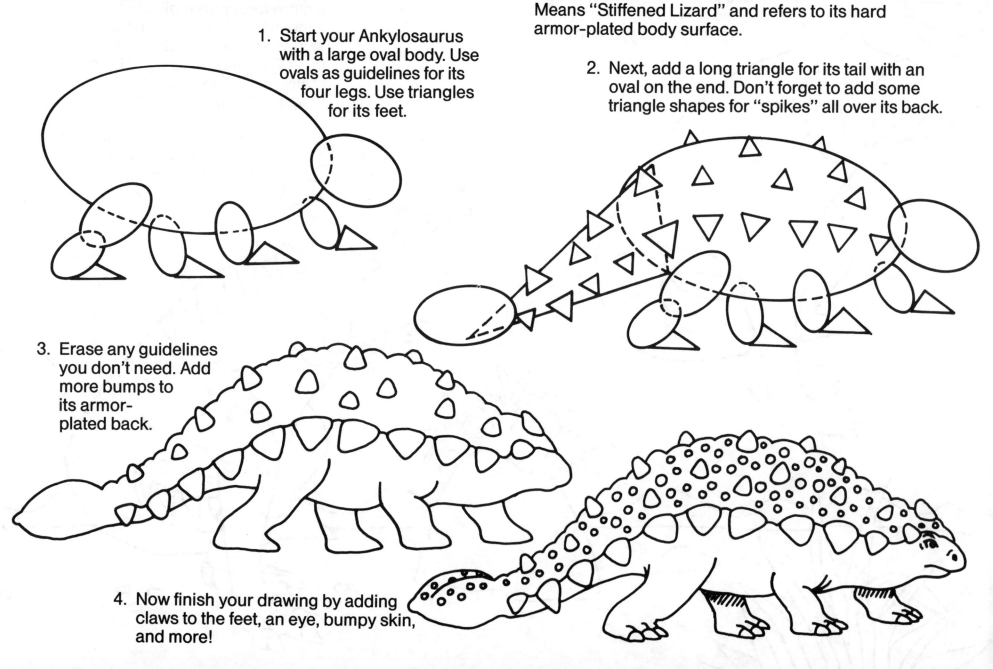

Pteranodon

(teh-RAN-o-don)

Means "Winged and Toothless" because it could fly and had no teeth.

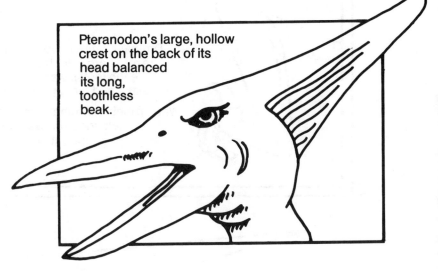

Pteranodon's large, hollow crest on the back of its head balanced its long, toothless beak.

1. Start your drawing with simple shapes. Pteranodon had a 25-foot wingspan, so be sure to draw its wings much longer than its body.

2. Next, draw guideline shapes for the legs, arms, and claws.

3. Erase all unnecessary lines and add lots of details.

Dromaeosaurus

(drom-ee-uh-SAWR-us)

Means "Swift Lizard" because this fast, fierce dinosaur ran upright on powerful hind legs.

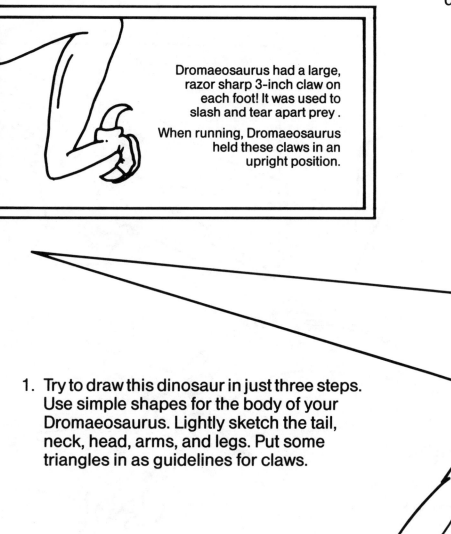

Dromaeosaurus had a large, razor sharp 3-inch claw on each foot! It was used to slash and tear apart prey.

When running, Dromaeosaurus held these claws in an upright position.

1. Try to draw this dinosaur in just three steps. Use simple shapes for the body of your Dromaeosaurus. Lightly sketch the tail, neck, head, arms, and legs. Put some triangles in as guidelines for claws.

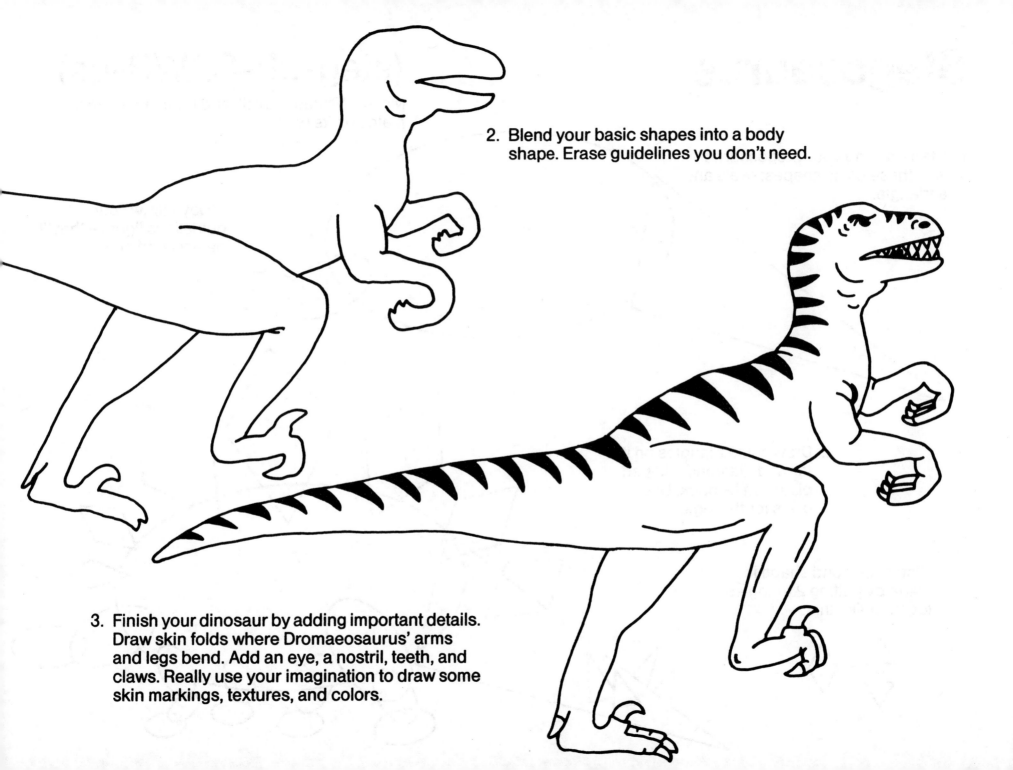

2. Blend your basic shapes into a body shape. Erase guidelines you don't need.

3. Finish your dinosaur by adding important details. Draw skin folds where Dromaeosaurus' arms and legs bend. Add an eye, a nostril, teeth, and claws. Really use your imagination to draw some skin markings, textures, and colors.

Stegosaurus

(steg-uh-SAWR-us)

Means "Plated Lizard" and refers to the rows of plates on its back.

1. Start drawing your Stegosaurus with these basic shapes: ovals and a triangle.

Always draw your guidelines lightly—they'll be easier to erase.

2. Draw some triangles on its tail and diamond-shaped plates on its back. Use ovals for the legs.

Hint: a diamond shape is made by putting 2 triangles together like this:

△ + ▽ = ◇

3. This step might look hard, but it's really easy. Take all your guidelines and blend them into a dinosaur shape. Erase any unnecessary lines so that you have a clean line drawing of your Stegosaurus.

Hint: the backplates are all a repeat of the diamond shape—some are hidden behind others.

4. Put the finishing touches on your drawing. Add texture to the backplates and some spots to Stegosaurus' back.

Saltopus

(SALT-o-pus)

Means "Leaping Foot" and refers to the way that Saltopus ran upright on its hind legs.

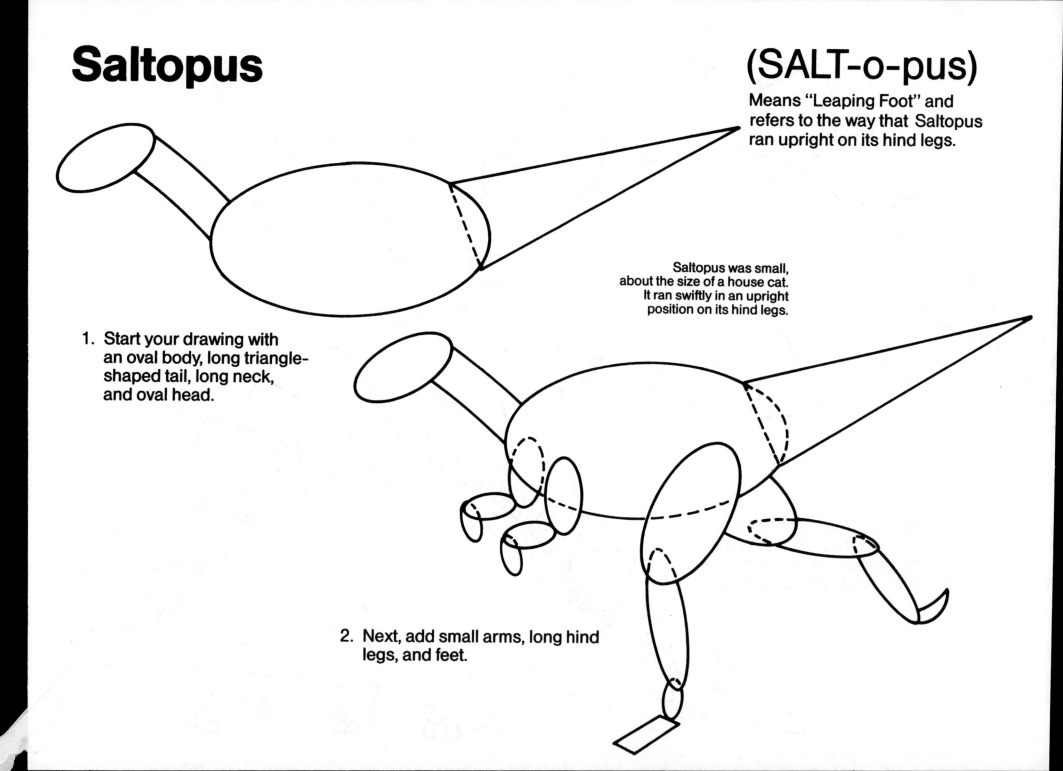

Saltopus was small, about the size of a house cat. It ran swiftly in an upright position on its hind legs.

1. Start your drawing with an oval body, long triangle-shaped tail, long neck, and oval head.

2. Next, add small arms, long hind legs, and feet.

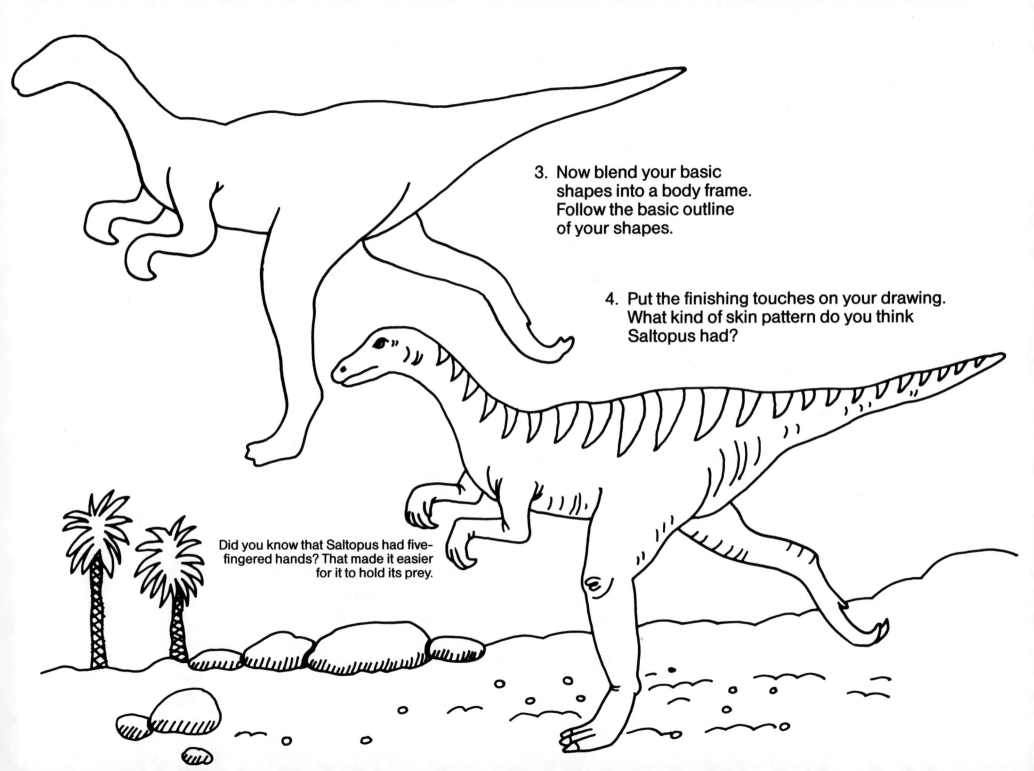

3. Now blend your basic shapes into a body frame. Follow the basic outline of your shapes.

4. Put the finishing touches on your drawing. What kind of skin pattern do you think Saltopus had?

Did you know that Saltopus had five-fingered hands? That made it easier for it to hold its prey.

Parasaurolophus (par-uh-SAWR-OL-uh-fus)

Means "Similiar-Crested Lizard."

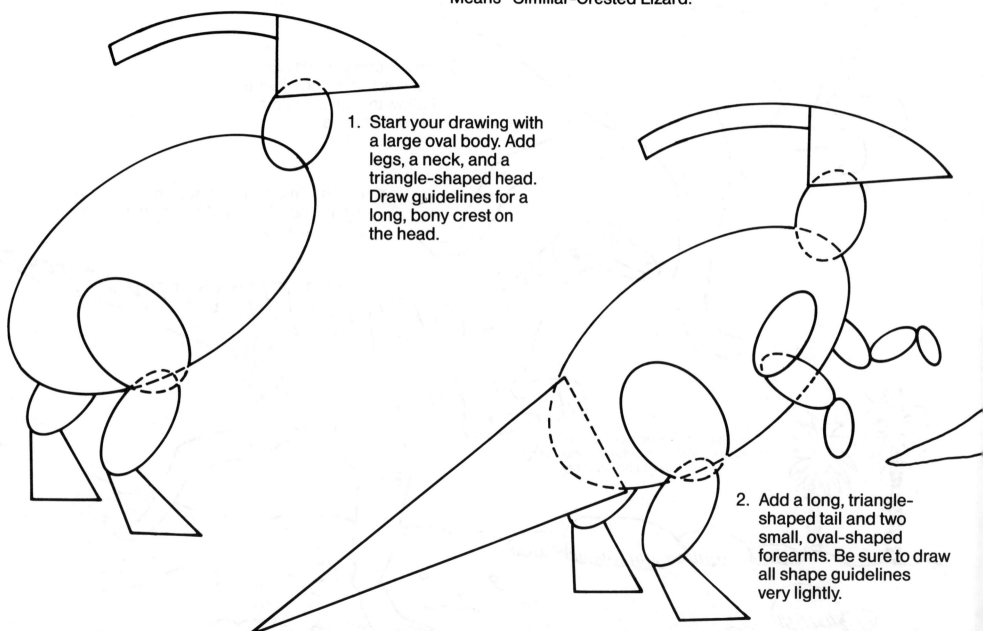

1. Start your drawing with a large oval body. Add legs, a neck, and a triangle-shaped head. Draw guidelines for a long, bony crest on the head.

2. Add a long, triangle-shaped tail and two small, oval-shaped forearms. Be sure to draw all shape guidelines very lightly.

3. Now blend all your guideline shapes into a body frame.

The purpose of the long, bony crest on the head of the Parasaurolophus is not known. Some scientists think the crest helped the animal's sense of smell. Others think the crest may have been used to make loud sounds.

4. Add claws, an eye, nostril, and lots of skin folds, shading, and texture.

Pachycephalosaurus
(pack-ee-SEF-al-owe-saw-rus)

Means "Reptile with a Thick Head" because the bone on top of its head was 10 inches thick!

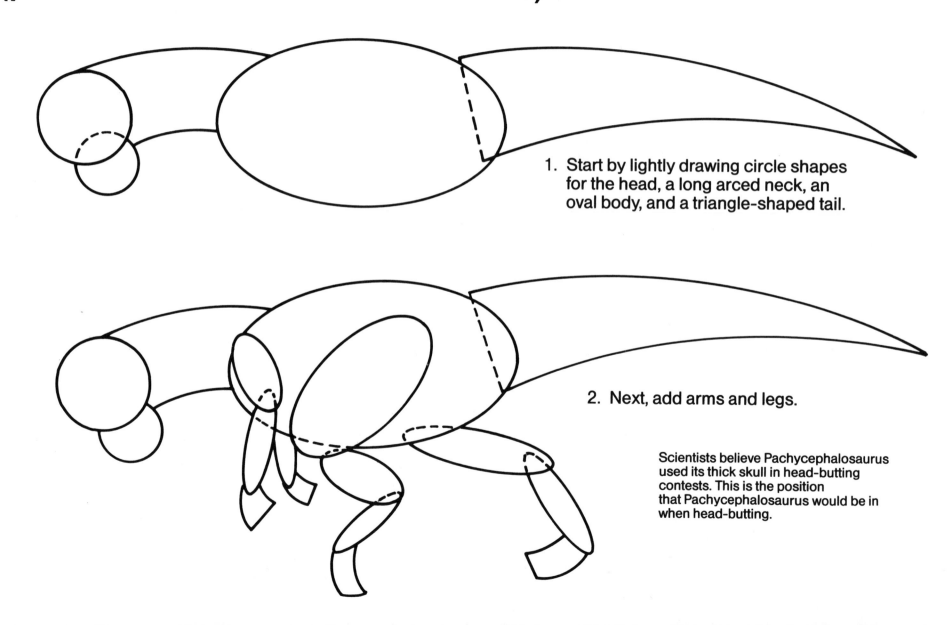

1. Start by lightly drawing circle shapes for the head, a long arced neck, an oval body, and a triangle-shaped tail.

2. Next, add arms and legs.

Scientists believe Pachycephalosaurus used its thick skull in head-butting contests. This is the position that Pachycephalosaurus would be in when head-butting.

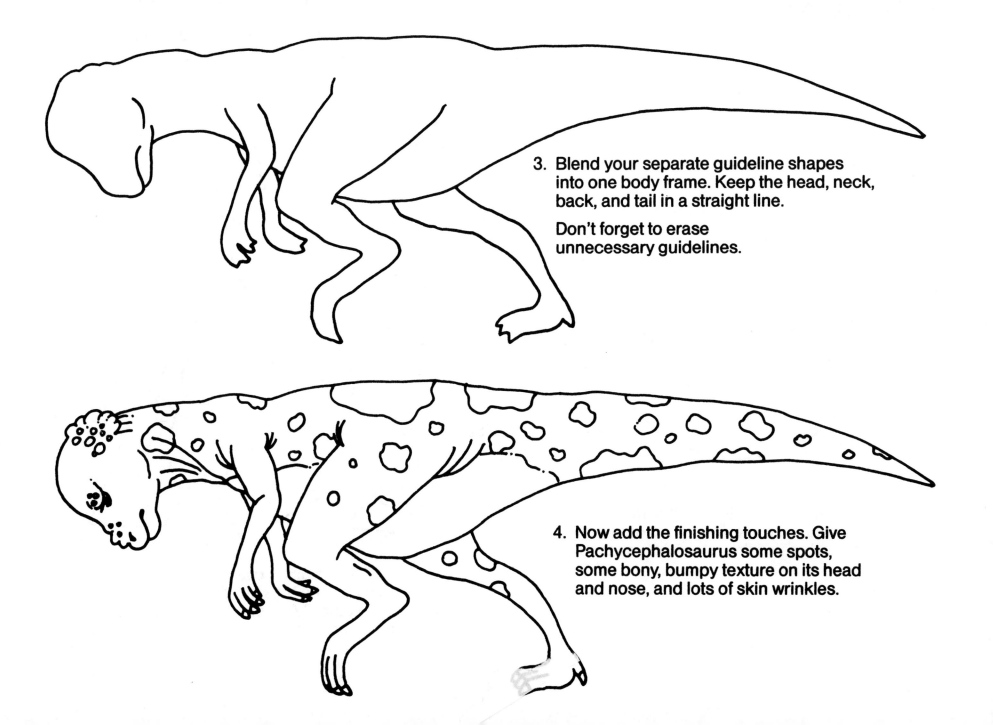

3. Blend your separate guideline shapes into one body frame. Keep the head, neck, back, and tail in a straight line.

Don't forget to erase unnecessary guidelines.

4. Now add the finishing touches. Give Pachycephalosaurus some spots, some bony, bumpy texture on its head and nose, and lots of skin wrinkles.

Triceratops

Means "Three-horned Face." It was one
of the last dinosaurs to become extinct.

1. Start drawing Triceratops using an oval,
   triangles, and a circle. It's easy to draw anything
   when you break it down to simple shapes!

2. Add 4 legs using oval and triangle shapes.
   See how the legs bend where the shapes meet
   each other? Add some triangles around the back
   of the head, too.

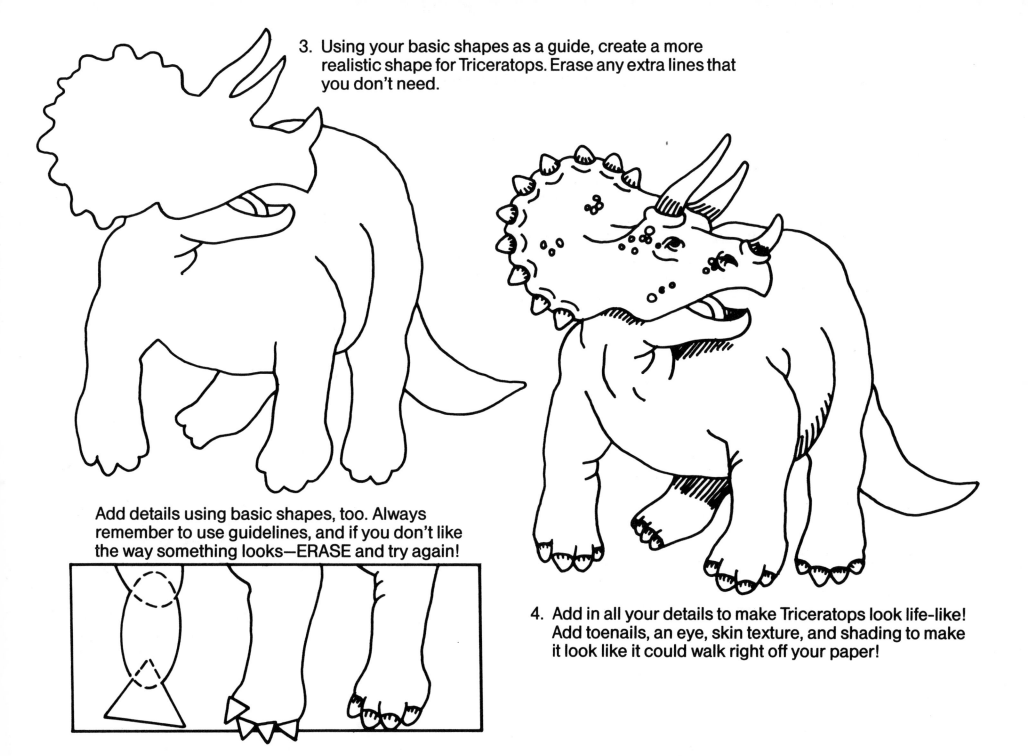

3. Using your basic shapes as a guide, create a more realistic shape for Triceratops. Erase any extra lines that you don't need.

Add details using basic shapes, too. Always remember to use guidelines, and if you don't like the way something looks—ERASE and try again!

4. Add in all your details to make Triceratops look life-like! Add toenails, an eye, skin texture, and shading to make it look like it could walk right off your paper!

Spinosaurus
(SPY-no-saw-rus)

Means "Spiny Lizard" and refers to the very long spines on this dinosaur's back.

1. Lightly draw the head, neck, body, and tail. Use basic shapes as your guideline.

2. Add arms, legs, and a guideline for the row of spines on Spinosaurus' back. Keep your guidelines light.

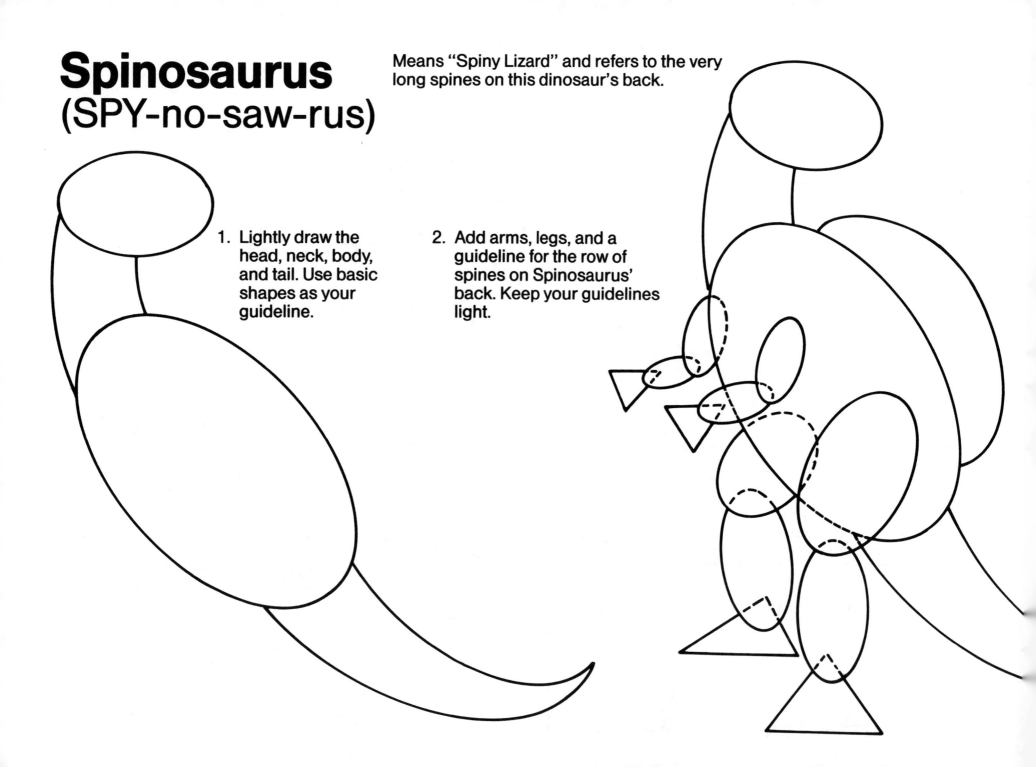

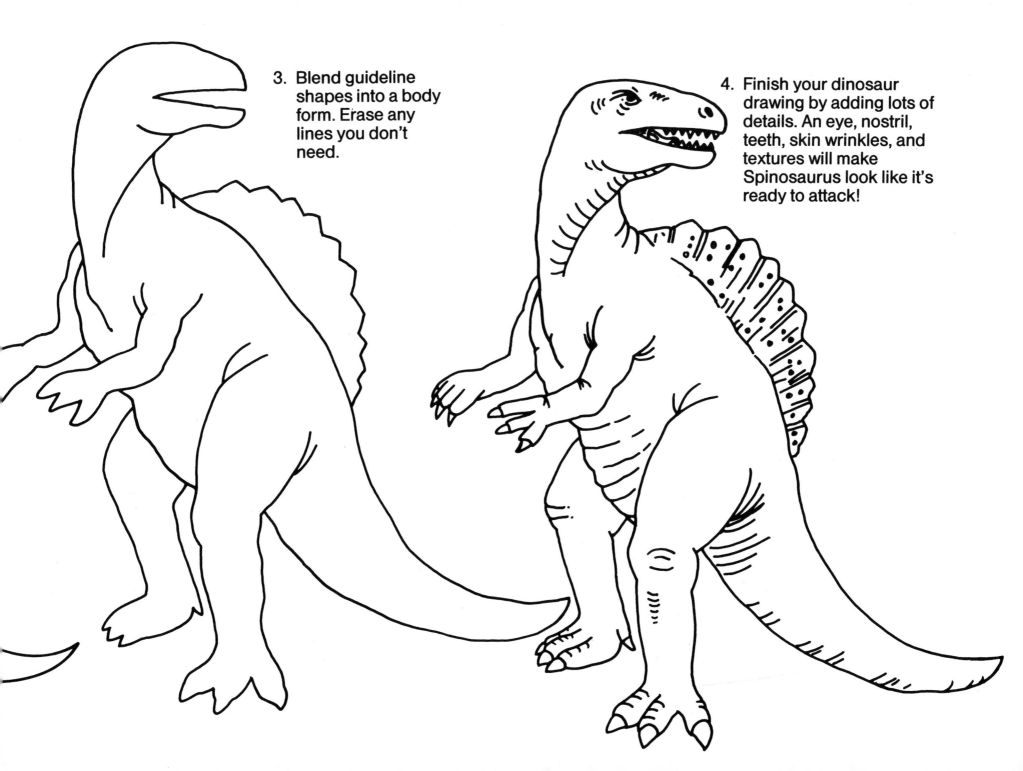

3. Blend guideline shapes into a body form. Erase any lines you don't need.

4. Finish your dinosaur drawing by adding lots of details. An eye, nostril, teeth, skin wrinkles, and textures will make Spinosaurus look like it's ready to attack!

Coelophysis
(see-lo-FISE-iss)

Means "Hollow Form" and refers to its hollow bones.

2. Blend your shapes into a body form. Add a long, slender tail. Erase any extra lines you don't need.

1. Start your drawing with basic shapes for the head, neck, body, arms, and legs.

3. Finish your drawing by adding details, such as an eye and claws. Color Coelophysis in bright colors with interesting skin designs.